CALLED
TO LEAD

A Handbook for Lay Leaders

Mark D. Johns

Augsburg Fortress
Minneapolis

CALLED TO LEAD
A Handbook for Lay Leaders

Developed in cooperation with the Division for Congregational Ministries of the Evangelical Lutheran Church in America, Michael R. Rothaar, project manager.

Editors: Laurie J. Hanson and James Satter

Cover design and series logo: Marti Naughton
Text design: James Satter
Cover photograph: Gordon Gray, FRPS

About the cover image: The centerpiece of the Resurrection Window in First Lisburn Presbyterian Church, Northern Ireland, was created by stained glass artist James Watson, Belfast, from fragments of church windows destroyed by a car bomb in 1981 and restored after a second bomb in 1989. The window symbolizes new life in Christ, which transforms darkness to light, hatred to love, despair to hope, and death to life. The members of First Lisburn Presbyterian have lived out this promise through new initiatives for community service, reconciliation, and peace-making.

ISBN 0-8066-4412-5

Manufactured in the U.S.A.

06   05   04   03   02   1   2   3   4   5   6   7   8   9   10

✠ Contents

A Congratulatory Note

(and what this book will do for you)

> You are to work together with other members to see that the
> worship and work of Christ are done in this congregation, and that
> God's will is done in this community and in the whole world.
>
> Installation of Elected Parish Officers,
> *Occasional Services: A Companion to Lutheran Book of Worship,*
> Augsburg Fortress, 1982, p. 134

Congratulations! You have been elected or appointed to a position of leadership in your congregation. You may have heard others jokingly (or perhaps even seriously) talk about your term of office as a duty, burden, or even punishment. Maybe your job seems impossible to you right now. After all, who can see "that God's will is done . . . in the whole world"? What a tall order!

But your election or appointment is really a high honor. It means that others in your congregation have seen in you the gifts and abilities they value among leaders. It is also an opportunity to serve God and the members of your congregation in an important and significant way. So approach this task as the affirmation and the opportunity that it is!

This book is designed to help you understand your calling as a congregational leader by providing information about your congregation and its relationship with the wider church, as well as equipping you with some basic tools and strategies for carrying out your responsibilities. Along the way, additional resources will be suggested so that you can find out more as you grow in your calling.

PART I

Called to Lead

*Your election or appointment to
a position of leadership in your congregation
is an expression of the baptismal calling.*

6

Chapter One

Called by Baptism

[Baptism] signifies that the old creature in us with all sins and evil desires is to be drowned and die through daily contrition and repentance, and on the other hand that daily a new person is to come forth and rise up to live before God in righteousness and purity forever.

Robert Kolb and Timothy J. Wengert, Small Catechism,

The Book of Concord: The Confessions of the Evangelical Lutheran Church,

Augsburg Fortress, 2000, p. 360

There is no calling higher than the calling that Christians receive in Holy Baptism. During the 16th century, Martin Luther made this clear in the Small Catechism, as well as in many of his other writings. No matter what we do in life, we are called through baptism into a unique relationship with God. We live out this relationship with God, day by day, in whatever work we do.

Centuries ago, ordinary people often did not believe that they could pray to God directly. Instead, they would ask a priest to approach the altar and pray for them. The phrase "priesthood of all believers" attempts to express the idea that all baptized people are sons and daughters of God, free to call upon God directly at any time or any place, and serving God—not just in church—but in all walks of life, every day. Martin Luther did not come up with "the priesthood of all believers" on his own. In developing this idea, he drew insights from several Bible passages, including these:

- "The one who believes and is baptized will be saved" (Mark 16:16).

- "When you were buried with him in baptism, you were also raised with him through faith in the power of God, who raised him from the dead" (Colossians 2:12).
- "He saved us, not because of any works of righteousness that we had done, but according to his mercy, through the water of rebirth and renewal by the Holy Spirit. This Spirit he poured out on us richly through Jesus Christ our Savior, so that, having been justified by his grace, we might become heirs according to the hope of eternal life" (Titus 3:5-7).

If you were baptized when you were an infant or young child, you probably do not remember the actual baptismal ceremony. But simply knowing you have been baptized is a powerful assurance of God's love for you. Luther suggested that Christians keep evidence of their baptisms close at hand. For some people, this may mean digging out a yellowed certificate, long ago stuffed away in a drawer or closet. For others, it may mean contacting another congregation in some distant place and requesting confirmation of the baptismal record. Still others may have some memento of the event —a Bible, necklace, cross, napkin, dress, or candle—that helps them reflect on the significance of the moment when they became members of the family of God. Whatever the reminder, the important fact is that God calls us to a special set of tasks and opportunities in the kingdom.

A promise and a commission

Baptism is both a promise and a commission. As a promise, baptism assures us of God's love and of our place in God's family. The words quoted at the beginning of this chapter assure us that no matter what failures we experience, each day we may turn to God in repentance and be made new through God's forgiveness. Baptism is our assurance of forgiveness. Baptism reminds us that as we grow in years, we mature in our understanding of what we have received from God. With that continued growth in faith, we develop the gifts and abilities God has given us and explore ever more challenging ways to live lives of service to God and God's people. In baptism, we receive the full abundance of God's gifts. But over time, we discover and develop these gifts as mature Christians.

Remember that you are a child of God.

Your election or appointment to a position of leadership in your congregation is an expression of the baptismal calling. Because of the doctrine of "the priesthood of all believers," you are holy, worthy, and fit to hold such a position of responsibility.

Furthermore, your peers in the congregation have seen in you the abilities necessary for leadership. They believe that you have developed the gifts that God has given you, and that you have grown in your faith and matured in your serving to the point that you are now ready to take on these important responsibilities. As you begin, you have both the affirmation of God and the affirmation of the members of your congregation. With God and your peers behind you to give you strength, encouragement, and support, you have the resources necessary to carry out your assigned duties. Remember that you are a child of God.

Chapter Two

Discerning
Gifts of the Spirit

For in the one Spirit we were all baptized into one body—Jews or
Greeks, slaves or free—and we were all made to drink of one Spirit.
Indeed, the body does not consist of one member but of many.
. . . Now you are the body of Christ and individually members of
it. And God has appointed in the church first apostles, second
prophets, third teachers; then deeds of power, then gifts of healing,
forms of assistance, forms of leadership, various kinds of tongues.

1 Corinthians 12:13-14, 27-28

The apostle Paul wrote letters to various congregations of the
first Christians, and a number of these letters have become a part of
the New Testament in our Bible. Again and again, Paul's letters stress
the idea that through baptism each Christian has certain gifts that
contribute to the ongoing work of the church. We do not all have
the same gifts and abilities, and some people may possess more gifts
than others, but no one has all of the gifts necessary to be the church
by himself or herself.

Working together, we each contribute the gifts we have, and only
by combining what each person brings is the congregation able to
carry out its mission and ministry. Thus, leadership in the church is
never a matter left to any one individual. Leadership belongs to the
entire family of faith, and it grows out of mutual cooperation and
sharing of abilities.

Many gifts, one body

In 1 Corinthians 12, Paul uses the metaphor of the human body to explain how members of the church work together for the common good. Paul points out the chaos that would result if the entire body were an eye, a hand, or a foot—and he calls attention to the equally chaotic result if some vital organ should happen to be cut off from the body. Each part of the body has its unique function, and the body is not complete unless each part functions as it should.

In the same way, your congregation requires a number of leadership functions in order to effectively carry out its mission and ministry. No one can do it all. As an elected or appointed leader in your congregation, your unique abilities and your special functions are vital to your congregation's success.

The role of the pastor

When introduced to ideas such as the priesthood of all believers, and the metaphor of the parts of the body, some people will begin to question the role of the pastor. If we are all priests with equal access to God because of our baptism, and if no one has all of the gifts necessary for the leadership of the congregation, why are we paying this person?

Certainly, without the rest of the congregation and the gifts of each member, the pastor would be lost. And the calling to be a pastor is no better or more significant than the calling to be a business executive, mechanic, or garbage collector. Yet, pastors have a unique role in the leadership of the congregation. First, they are called to proclaim God's word and administer the sacraments. Because pastors in the Evangelical Lutheran Church in America (ELCA) and most traditional denominations have had their gifts and fitness for service carefully examined and scrutinized by the wider church, they link congregations to the traditions, practices, and beliefs of Christians in other times and places. Because pastors must complete extensive special training—first by completing college and then usually by spending an additional four years in seminary classroom and practical studies—pastors bring a special collection of gifts to the congregations they serve.

By virtue of his or her training and experience, and not by virtue of extra holiness or a special relationship with God, the pastor holds a particular position of leadership as the congregation's resident theologian, primary teacher, worship leader, and evangelist. Finally, because the pastor devotes his or her full attention to the concerns of the congregation and the needs of its members, the pastor has a unique perspective on the ministry challenges and opportunities the congregation faces. Thus, the role of the pastor as leader, teacher, and guide should be respected in the congregation as essential to ministry.

But even with this specialized training, pastors are not "cookie cutter" clones of each other. Every pastor has a unique set of gifts and abilities. For example, some pastors are gifted administrators, while others find their strength in music or worship leadership. Some pastors are extremely effective counselors, while others are particularly gifted in leading groups in study and prayer. Some pastors have particular strengths in working with children and youth, while others are extremely effective in meeting the spiritual needs of the elderly. No two pastors have exactly the same set of gifts. Even though certain minimum competencies must be developed in a wide range of areas before a person is ordained as a pastor, it is essential that members of the congregation bring their gifts to completely fulfill the congregation's ministry.

Whomever a congregation calls as its pastor, the congregation will not receive a Superman or Superwoman. It will be necessary for lay leaders to bring their gifts to fill the voids that remain. Also, a change in pastors will inevitably bring changes in the gifts that must be supplied by lay leaders. As vital as the pastor's role may be, it is always the case that the full range of gifts necessary for the functioning of the congregation must be supplied, not by a single individual, but by many members and leaders living, working, and sharing together in a community of faith.

Your gifts

So what gifts do *you* bring as you begin your leadership role in the congregation? You have many gifts, and you may discover in the course of your service that you have some you did not suspect you had. But let's take stock of those of which you are aware right now. In the Bible passage below, the apostle Paul lists a number of possible gifts:

> Now there are varieties of gifts, but the same Spirit; and there are varieties of services, but the same Lord; and there are varieties of activities, but it is the same God who activates all of them in everyone. To each is given the manifestation of the Spirit for the common good. To one is given through the Spirit the utterance of wisdom, and to another the utterance of knowledge according to the same Spirit, to another faith by the same Spirit, to another gifts of healing by the one Spirit, to another the working of miracles, to another prophecy, to another the discernment of spirits, to another various kinds of tongues, to another the interpretation of tongues. All these are activated by one and the same Spirit, who allots to each one individually just as the Spirit chooses.

> 1 Corinthians 12:4-11

How do we translate Paul's ancient terms into gifts we might recognize today? Look at other people in your congregation for examples of the gifts. Then consider how each gift might be yours. For example, Paul mentions the gifts of speaking and interpreting other tongues. A congregation situated in a community with a population of recent immigrants might benefit greatly from individuals in the congregation with the gift of being able to speak, read, or write Spanish. Is this a gift you share? Is there a similar gift you have or might develop? Perhaps or perhaps not, but there will be other gifts you do have! Begin to inventory your own unique gifts here, and be on the lookout for still more that become apparent over time.

After completing the chart on page 14 for yourself, seek feedback from another member of your congregation. Does this person agree that the gifts you have identified are indeed your strengths? Does this person see other gifts in you that you have not identified? Once you stop to consider them, are you surprised by the number of gifts you have for leadership in your congregation? Are you amazed at the wide range of gifts you can see among the members of your congregation?

In the gifts for the church poured out in baptismal waters, the abundance of God's generosity is overwhelming. Everything we need has been given us in that act of water and God's word. It is simply up to us to recognize, develop, and use that which is already ours. No single individual—not even the pastor—has a complete range of gifts. With everyone who makes up the community of faith, and the gifts that all contribute together, God's church and your congregation are abundantly blessed.

In the next chapter, you will have the opportunity to explore some of the realities your congregation faces, and to consider further how your gifts can be applied to meet the challenges that exist.

Additional resources

Our Gifts: Identifying and Developing Leaders, by David Mayer (Minneapolis: Augsburg Fortress, 2002).

Paul's term for the gift	Ways this gift appears in people in our congregation	Ways this gift is mine
Wisdom		
Knowledge		
Faith		
Healing		
Miracles		
Prophecy		
Tongues		
Discernment		

This chart is adapted from p. 20 of *God's Family*, by John W. Hattery, a unit of the "Catechetics for Today" curriculum edited by Johns Stevens Kerr, ©1980 by Parish Life Press, Philadelphia.

PART II

Your Place in the Congregation

To succeed as a leader in
such a complex organization requires
knowledge, actions, and character.

Chapter Three

Just What Is
a Congregation?

A congregation is a community of baptized persons whose existence depends on the proclamation of the Gospel and the admin-
istration of the sacraments and whose purpose is to worship God,
to nurture its members, and to reach out in witness and service to
the world. To this end it assembles regularly for worship and nurture, organizes and carries out ministry to its people and neighborhood, and cooperates with and supports the wider church to strive
for the fulfillment of God's mission in the world.

Constitution of the Evangelical Lutheran Church in America,
edition revised as of August 13, 2001, provision 9.11.

All human organizations have certain qualities in common.
Whether it happens to be the local garden club, the Red Cross, or an
order of monks living in an abbey, any group of people who gather
together for some specific purpose will share certain characteristics.
The local church where you now are a leader is a rather complex
group, because it shares the characteristics of at least three distinct
types of human organizations. Your congregation shares much with
the garden club, the Red Cross, and the monks—all at the same time!

Voluntary association

Like the garden club, your congregation is a type of organization
known as a "voluntary association." Because individuals choose to

belong to your congregation and are free to choose how involved they will become and how much time they will spend in congregational activities, they are said to associate with one another voluntarily. Voluntary associations usually have a single, rather specific focus. For the garden club the focus is gardening. For the antique car club the focus is old cars. As a voluntary association, the focus for a congregation is Christian fellowship.

For more information, see *Our Context: Exploring Our Congregation and Community,* including the "Congregational Model" diagram on page 104 of that book.

Any voluntary association, including your congregation, must pay particular attention to involving the widest possible participation of members in setting goals so that the central focus is not lost. Further, when making key decisions, voluntary associations must work to build a consensus among members so that factions do not develop. These organizations also must be intentional about deepening relationships among members through fellowship, visitation, and social engagement so that members will continue to choose to associate with one another. Voluntary associations must manage conflicts creatively and must constantly be open to new individuals who wish to join. Above all, voluntary associations must create effective lines of communication among members, and particularly between leaders and members. Because members associate voluntarily, they can choose to stop associating if not fully included, and when that happens, the group ceases to exist.

If your organization is just a club or voluntary association with a hobby or interest at its center, there is already quite a list of things to keep in mind. But your congregation is all this and more.

Non-profit organization

Like the local chapter of the Red Cross, your congregation is a non-profit organization. It is incorporated, which means that it must meet certain legal requirements for maintaining bylaws and electing a board of directors. It is a tax-exempt entity, and therefore it must meet state and federal government standards for receiving, accounting for, and acknowledging contributions. It has to establish and follow certain organizational procedures for making decisions, keeping records, and using formal communication methods to disseminate legal notices to voting members. If your congregation owns a building and property, it must comply with local ordinances concerning zoning, construction standards, and fire safety. Property ownership and corporate status also mean that a congregation must insure itself against various liabilities. Insurers may require that a congregation establishes additional procedures, writes and formally adopts policy statements, and installs certain safety equipment to reduce exposure to risks of lawsuits or other claims.

Not every voluntary association becomes a non-profit organization, and not every non-profit organization is a voluntary association. But your congregation is both. Most congregations, even the smallest, are too large and have ministries too complex to allow them to remain as informal associations. The more formal status of non-profit corporation adds complications, but also protects the congregation and its members from many legal and fiscal dangers. This corporate status offers greater stability and official recognition. But to achieve this security and acknowledgment for the congregation, leaders must do what the law and good corporate operating procedures demand. These requirements are generally not difficult, but they require a certain amount of awareness, time, and attention.

Community of spiritual formation

In addition to being a voluntary association and a non-profit organization, your congregation has a third dimension as a community of faith dedicated to the worship of God, education about the basics of Christianity, evangelical witness, service, and the lifelong spiritual growth of members. Like monks in an abbey, your congregation is a "community of spiritual formation." It is dedicated to living out the faith authentically in prayer and service, and to passing that faith on to others through witness and teaching.

In this regard, your congregation is even more than the garden club or the Red Cross. Yet, as a community of spiritual formation, your congregation does not cease to be a voluntary association and a non-profit organization. It is all three at once. The congregation's role as community of spiritual formation should determine the way in which it acts as a voluntary association and as a non-profit organization, but it does not replace these roles. The congregation continues to function as all three.

This is not a new situation for the church. In the Bible, the story of the early Christians is full of admonitions to members of ancient congregations to live and work in harmony with one another and in conformity with the laws of government. In the book of Acts, for example, we read that the first Christian congregation in Jerusalem struggled with matters of organization and procedure, and it was concerned with handling finances in ways that would be above reproach. From the earliest days of Christianity, congregations have had to juggle the multiple roles of voluntary association, non-profit organization, and community of spiritual formation. That juggling act has become more complicated as our society has grown more complex, but the essential nature of congregations has not changed in 2,000 years.

The role of congregational leaders

Because the congregation operates as three distinct types of organizations, its leaders must develop knowledge, skills, and practices that are, at once, appropriate to all three organizational types. Thus, congregational leaders must—first and foremost—be spiritual people, committed to their faith in Christ, eager to continue growing in their personal spiritual formation, and anxious to assist others in their growth. At the same time, congregational leaders must be knowledgeable of policies and procedures required of non-profit corporations under the laws of the land and the best operating practices available. Without neglecting these other requirements, congregational leaders must also be skilled in deepening relationships, building consensus, managing conflicts, and communicating effectively as leaders of a voluntary association.

Fortunately, while each elected or appointed leader must understand the requirements for multiple forms of leadership, it is not essential for each leader be an expert in every aspect. Some leaders have gifts for developing the kinds of relationships necessary to maintain the congregation as a healthy voluntary association. Some are gifted at maintaining the lines of communication that such an organization requires. Other leaders have extensive training and experience in the legal and procedural matters necessary to maintain a non-profit organization. Still others have skills in accounting or financial management critical to organizational success. Some leaders are excellent teachers or mentors, while others excel at prayer or music for worship. What is essential is that all congregational leaders have a passion for the faith and a desire to contribute their gifts, which all build the community of spiritual formation.

But equally essential is a mutual appreciation of why all of these gifts are necessary and how complicated a congregation truly is. Otherwise, when responding to any situation, some people will suggest responding in ways appropriate to a voluntary association, while others insist on responding in ways appropriate to a non-profit organization, and still others object and say that people are forgetting to act like "real" Christians. Without adequate understanding of the complex nature of the congregation, leaders will not have the insights needed to see all sides of the argument—the gifts of some people will be acclaimed, while the gifts of others are devalued.

Knowledge, actions, and character

To succeed as a leader in such a complex organization requires knowledge, actions, and character. That is, leaders must know some things, do some things, and simply be some things. However, they need not all know, do, and be the *same* things!

For example, those who handle the congregation's financial affairs must know some basic principles of accounting and applicable laws. They must be able to organize systems for receiving and recording monetary offerings and gifts, and they must be honest in all of their dealings with cash and accounts. On the other hand, those who teach Sunday school need to know the intellectual abilities of children at each age and what biblical and theological concepts are appropriate to teach at various developmental levels. They need skills in classroom management and teaching techniques, and they must be patient and loving examples for their students.

Additional resources

Our Context: Exploring Our Congregation and Community, by Mark D. Johns (Minneapolis: Augsburg Fortress, 2002).

Our Gifts: Identifying and Developing Leaders, by David P. Mayer (Minneapolis: Augsburg Fortress, 2002).

Our Mission: Discovering God's Call to Us, by Robin and John McCullough-Bade (Minneapolis: Augsburg Fortress, 2002).

Our Stewardship: Managing Our Assets, by John Golv (Minneapolis: Augsburg Fortress, 2002).

Chapter Four

Rules of the Road

Each congregation shall have governing documents . . .

Constitution of the Evangelical Lutheran Church in America, provision 9.53.

Because of the complex nature of the congregation and the challenges faced by those who lead it, it's important that members and leaders agree about how the congregation will function. Indeed, certain documents are required, either by the laws of the state or by the churchwide organization or denomination. Those people with particular gifts for the non-profit corporation aspect of the congregation's life will, perhaps, best understand the need to document these agreements in an orderly fashion. But these agreements ultimately affect all areas of congregational life. The official documents of the congregation not only serve legal and organizational functions, but they also define the common purpose of the voluntary association and specify the faith that the community shares.

All members should have access to the governing documents of the congregation. A current copy should be on public file in the congregation's office or perhaps in its library. As an elected or appointed leader, you should have access to these documents and become familiar with their contents.

Constitutions

A constitution contains the fundamental agreements of a congregation. State laws usually require that a constitution or a document very much like it be maintained by any corporation within the state.

Most denominations, including the Evangelical Lutheran Church in America (ELCA), also require congregations to maintain such a document. Constitutions embody those agreements among congregational members that are so basic that they are not likely to change very frequently. For example, the name of the congregation and a statement of the basic Christian doctrines upheld by its members are not subject to revision very often. Therefore, the constitution is written in a way that makes it somewhat difficult to alter. Further, any alterations require a process that is lengthy enough to provide time for a good deal of deliberation.

Your congregation does not exist in isolation. It is but one small part of the body of Christ. Many of the agreements embodied in the constitution have to do with how **Your congregation does not exist in isolation.** your congregation will relate to the wider church—that is, how this congregation will relate to other congregations which share its beliefs and are united with it in common mission. Because a constitution is largely an agreement between the members of one congregation and the members of all other congregations of the same denomination, the ELCA asks that its congregations adopt many constitutional provisions that are shared by all other congregations of the ELCA. Further, as part of the deliberative process, it asks that any changes to the constitution of a congregation be sent to the secretary of the synod. This makes it possible for others who have a stake in these decisions to be aware of them and, collectively through the synod, to have an opportunity to voice objections or ratify the change.

Some provisions of the constitution, however, are strictly of local concern. Matters regarding how often congregational meetings will be held, how many voting members will make for a quorum, how many people will be elected to the congregation council, how officers are selected, and what standing committees the congregation will have are all important and not subject to frequent change. However, they are local concerns and may vary from congregation to congregation. These decisions, too, may be recorded in the constitution.

Constitutions also include provisions that one hopes never will be enacted, as they provide vital protections for the congregation in times of crisis. These include articles concerning the discipline of members who become disruptive or who promote beliefs contrary to the doctrines of faith. Here, too, are procedures that must be followed in order to dismiss a pastor and limitations spelling out the specific circumstances in which such action might be justified. A process for dissolving the agreements with other congregations and withdrawing from the denomination may also be outlined, a process designed to protect faithful Christians from being robbed of congregational property by deceptive or manipulative individuals, while still respecting the congregation's right to choose how it lives out its faith. While such provisions seldom are necessary, they need to be in place before a crisis erupts. These safeguards should be set up so they are not easy to change by a small group of members at a time when passions are inflamed.

The constitution of the congregation can only be altered if amendments are approved by a majority vote at a properly called and conducted congregational meeting, and then ratified by a two-thirds majority at the next annual meeting of the congregation. Therefore, it requires two successive votes over a period of at least several weeks—or often up to one year—with written notice of the proposed decision provided to all voting members, before constitutional provisions may be changed. This allows for thoughtful deliberation and the opportunity for all to participate in the decision.

Bylaws

Not every congregational decision or agreement between members needs to stand unchanged for a generation. In fact, some things ought to change occasionally. A healthy congregation is one that can adapt to new circumstances. Congregations adopt bylaws for this reason. Bylaws frequently provide details about how constitutional decisions should be carried out or outline procedures that might be subject to change more frequently than those in the constitution.

Most often, the bylaws and the constitution are incorporated into a single document. By way of illustration, in the *Model Constitution for Congregations of the Evangelical Lutheran Church in America*, the 10th chapter is concerned with congregational meetings. The suggested wording for the first article in this chapter is this:

C10.01. The [annual] [semi-annual] [quarterly] meeting of this congregation shall be held at a time specified in the bylaws.

The first thing that the congregation must decide, in following this model, is the frequency of regular congregational meetings. While most congregations hold only one such meeting each year, some hold two, and others have four. This is a constitutional decision. But once that decision is made, a bylaw probably would be inserted immediately following this article of the constitution, and it might look something like this:

C10.01.01. The annual meeting of the congregation will be held on the fourth Sunday of January at 1:00 P.M.

The number of the bylaw links it to the number of the article in the constitution, but adds another two digit number, indicating that this is the first (perhaps the only) bylaw relating to this particular constitutional provision. While the precise numbering system may vary, the idea is that bylaws are frequently recorded in the same document as the constitution and often elaborate or provide details on constitutional provisions.

A bylaw may be changed or deleted by a majority vote at any properly called congregational meeting. If at some future time the members of the congregation decide that they would prefer to move their annual meeting to the third Sunday of January (perhaps to avoid a conflict with the Super Bowl football game), the change easily could be made. The constitution stipulates the decision that is most basic: The voting members of this congregation will have a formal meeting perhaps once a year (or twice, or four times, if that's what the constitution says). But the details are left to the bylaws. So long as the bylaws don't conflict with the constitution, the congregation may easily change them from time to time as seems appropriate.

Bylaws are also handy ways to preserve congregational decisions in an orderly manner and record them in a central location. If some time next year members of the congregation council try to recall when the annual meeting is supposed to be held—and some council members recollect that it is to be on the third Sunday of January, but others remember that the fourth Sunday in January was decided —the secretary should be able to quickly turn to the bylaws to look up the decision. No one has to depend on memory. Whenever it is anticipated that a decision made by congregational vote is to stand from year to year, and yet may be subject to change a few years down the road, it's a good idea to have it approved in the form of a bylaw.

Continuing resolutions

Decisions made at congregational meetings are not the only ones that need to be remembered over time. The congregation council is the legal board of directors of the congregation, as well as the group responsible for maintaining the integrity of the community of spiritual formation and for enlivening the fellowship of members in the voluntary association. It also makes policy decisions that stand for long periods of time. These decisions should be recorded in an orderly fashion. Job descriptions, personnel policies, and details about organizational structure need to be determined, put on record, and communicated to those affected. The documents used for these purposes are called "continuing resolutions." Continuing resolutions are adopted or changed at any properly called meeting of the congregation council by a vote of two-thirds of the members.

On what holidays will the church office close and the church secretary receive holiday pay? After five years of service, how many weeks of vacation does the custodian receive? Which family-leave policy applies for the part-time organist? What is the official job description of the choir director? All of these are questions that should be answered by policy decisions. The congregation council might make new policies as each situation comes up. In fairness, however, the policies should remain in place over time and apply equally to all until they there is need for the policy to be changed. So when a policy is set, it can be approved in the form of a resolution that continues until it is changed or terminated.

Continuing resolutions also are an ideal way for the congregation council to establish various ongoing functional committees or task groups that are not specified by the constitution or bylaws. The resolution can contain the name of the committee, the number of people serving on it, the way members are chosen, the length of terms of service, and a job description of what the committee is to accomplish. Similarly, such resolutions can be used as a means for the congregation council to provide details about the duties of particular individuals, such as outlining how cash receipts should be deposited by the treasurer, or the style in which minutes should be reported by the secretary.

Continuing resolutions usually are collected into a binder or other policy book and reviewed every few years, or as necessary, to make sure they are consistent with one another and with the constitution and bylaws presently in effect. This type of policy book often contains a copy of the current constitution and bylaws as well. Together, the governing documents of the congregation preserve important agreements over time, help to clear up disagreements or misunderstandings, and offer clear processes to follow in times of conflict or difficulty. Because of this, it is helpful to distribute a copy of the policy book to each member of the congregation council and other key leaders for easy reference. Not only are such documents legally required of a non-profit organization, but they also provide stability to the community of spiritual formation and unambiguous means of communicating common agreements to the members of the voluntary association. In short, maintaining the constitution, bylaws, and continuing resolutions well is essential for a smooth running and effective congregation of any size.

Additional resources

Our Context: Exploring Our Congregation and Community, by Mark D. Johns (Minneapolis: Augsburg Fortress, 2002).

Chapter Five

Your Unique Congregation

Each congregation shall structure itself in such a way as to involve its members in fulfilling the definition, purpose, and functions of a congregation.

Constitution of the Evangelical Lutheran Church in America, provision 9.51.

All groups of humans share certain characteristics, and all congregations—particularly those of the same denomination—share many things in common. But as similar as they are, no two congregations are exactly alike. Each one is unique, with its own history and traditions, its own practices and ways of doing things, and its own corporate personality.

A retired pastor who does a great deal of pulpit supply (filling in for pastors who are ill or vacationing) once remarked, "I preached in over 20 congregations last year. They were all within 100 miles of one another. They all belonged to the same denomination. And they all used the same worship books. But there weren't two of them that conducted their services in exactly the same way!"

These observations were only about the worship service. When we consider the possible variations in education programs, fellowship activities, committee structures, and all other aspects of parish life, it becomes clear just how different congregations can be from one another.

What accounts for these differences? How did they come about? Why is it important to understand them?

Habits and traditions—
"We've always done it this way"

Many of the characteristics that make congregations different from one another are really just habits that congregational members have developed over the years. Frequently, the origins of these practices are lost. Our ways of doing things in worship, in Sunday school, in men's, women's, or youth groups, or in various working groups or committees become standardized simply because they have always been done that way in the past. As with the congregation

O nce there was a congregation where everyone was taught, from the time they were young, to bow their heads as they entered the worship area. This tradition was enforced rigidly, and those who did not bow their heads as they entered the church nave would receive quite a scolding from other members.

One young man, who had come from another town, realized that this bowing was not practiced elsewhere and became determined to discover the origin of the practice. He asked many of the elders, but often was reprimanded for even asking such a thing. "It's tradition! It is what we do here, don't question it!" he was told.

Finally, the young man found the oldest member in the congregation—a man more than 100 years old who was homebound. The young man went to him and asked him, "Sir, why do the people in this congregation bow their heads as they enter the worship area?"

The old man replied, "Before the current church was built, we worshiped in the log cabin. The door frame on the cabin was very low, so those who did not lower their heads as they entered would bump them."

described one page 30, where the people bowed their heads as they entered worship, the origins may have been very practical at one time, but now may be humorous or out of date.

Just because a practice is a habit, however, does not necessarily mean it is unimportant or that it ought to be changed simply for change's sake. Habits often become traditions because they happen to work well in that particular setting. As long as a particular way of getting something done is working effectively and efficiently, following the habitual pattern avoids having to "reinvent the wheel." Congregational groups need not spend lots of time and energy planning from scratch if they can simply agree to "do it the same way we did last year." This isn't always bad.

Further, some habits or traditions take on special meaning for congregational members, and these should not be tampered with lightly. Clearly, for many of the people in that fictional congregation (on page 30), the act of bowing one's head upon entering the worship area had taken on spiritual significance. It was no longer a matter of avoiding bumping one's head, but had become a sign of respect for the One worshiped in that space. A practice that had begun for very practical reasons had become a tradition with greater meaning for those who passed it on. There is no benefit to challenging such traditions needlessly, particularly when they build up the faith of others.

On the other hand, habits can become problems when they outlive their usefulness. When a habit prevents the congregation from considering more effective ways of accomplishing the same things, the habit must be questioned. When a particular practice becomes divisive or causes conflict in the congregation, it may be time to abolish that tradition. While traditions are cherished, a congregation should be constantly alert to ways that habits may be holding the congregation back from more effective or innovative ways to achieve its mission.

Like nearly all other voluntary associations, congregations can be notoriously resistant to change. An old joke is that the seven last words of the church will be "We've never done it that way before!" While change for the sake of change is rather senseless, failure to change when a better way is offered is equally absurd. Leaders have a special duty to guard valuable traditions, but they also must be among the first people to challenge traditions that have outlived their usefulness and now impede the congregation's work. Leaders must pray for the wisdom to know the difference!

Congregational structures

Perhaps no other area of congregational life is more subject to habit than how the congregation structures itself to accomplish ministry. The way congregational tasks are assigned to various councils, committees, boards, or task groups is quickly institutionalized and, too often, difficult to change. A generation or two ago, many congregations were structured in identical ways, with a certain set of boards or committees, regardless of their size and circumstances. This structure often paralleled the structure of the denomination,

A small congregation consisting primarily of older adults, with a half dozen children in Sunday school, probably does not need a 12-member Board of Christian Education and a separate Youth Ministry Committee. An outdated constitution may stipulate that both should exist, but in the congregation's present circumstances this just wouldn't make sense. On the other hand, there may be nothing in the longstanding constitution about a committee for ministry with older adults, but this congregation would clearly have such ministries as a priority and should adapt its structure accordingly.

with each office having a corresponding group in each congregation. But congregational structure is not a "one size fits all" commodity.

How tasks are distributed within a congregation and what groups are appointed to carry them out depends on local circumstances. Ideally, structures are not difficult-to-change constitutional matters. Rather, they should be set out in continuing resolutions of the congregation council so that they may be flexible as needs change. At the very least, the most detailed job descriptions of each board or committee ought to be flexible in this way.

The old adage among architects applies also to congregations: "Form follows function." Your congregation should update its constitution and bylaws to allow for a flexible structure. Then, the structure put in place ought to meet the needs of current ministries. If a given committee or board seems not to have enough to do, eliminate it or combine it with another. If a ministry opportunity awaits, appoint a group to explore the possibilities. Be creative! The purpose of the church is not to create as many committees as possible. The organizational structure needs to be designed in a way that facilitates ministry, not in a way that makes ministry more difficult.

As a congregational leader, you may find yourself on one or more boards or committees. If the specific tasks of your committee are not clear, ask for further explanation from your congregation's officers or pastors. If a direct connection between your board's duties and the mission goals of the congregation is not obvious, seek clarification. If you think of a more efficient or effective way of accomplishing your tasks, by all means suggest it. Don't let "We've never done it that way before!" be the seven last words of *your* congregation!

Ethnic roots

A frequently overlooked source of traditions in a congregation is the particular history of the congregation and the attitudes that were established by its founding members. Even after many generations, certain attitudes and expectations that started with founding members can be alive and well in congregations today. This legacy is expressed in attitudes, expectations, and behaviors that are passed from one generation to the next. Even as people of other backgrounds join the congregation, over time they tend to adopt the congregation's pervasive culture as their own.

Different ethnic groups from Europe that founded congregations in North America had different sets of expectations of what it means to be the church. In addition to this, there were significant differences in expectations even within the same nationality. Germans who settled in Pennsylvania in the mid-1700s, for example, arrived for different reasons and brought different expectations than the Germans who settled in Iowa in the late 1800s.

Spend time researching the history of the congregation.

This historical influence finds expression in some unexpected ways. When it is pointed out, congregational members often react with surprise, not having realized how much effect the past may have on the present. For example, some Danish groups that came to the United States in the 1860s and 1870s had a strong tradition of participatory democracy, a belief that all decisions should be shared by all members. Today, congregations founded by these groups often continue to have quarterly congregational meetings rather than annual meetings. If asked why this is the case, members today might respond, "Because that's how it's always been done here." But the roots of the practice go back to the founders well over 100 years ago.

An interesting exercise for you as a congregational leader would be to spend time researching the history of the congregation. Who were the founders? What was their motivation for founding a new congregation? What were the circumstances and practices of the church body from which they came? What religious beliefs and practices, if any, were they protesting against?

Most congregations have a library where brief histories of the congregation have been preserved—often in books published at the time of a centennial or another significant anniversary of the congregation's founding. If such a history is not available, it is possible that some of the congregation's oldest members will have memories of stories told to them by parents or grandparents. Interviews with these older members, perhaps preserved on tape, can help you to begin assembling a congregational history if it does not exist or expand an existing historical record. This process also can help you to understand how the past makes your congregation a unique community today.

Additional resources

Our Structure: Carrying Out the Vision, by Brian H. Hughes (Minneapolis: Augsburg Fortress, 2002).

Video

Lutheran Roots in America, a MOSAIC video available through the ELCA Department for Communication (2002).

Web site

ELCA Archives: www.elca.org/os/archives/intro.html

PART III

Getting Help from the Neighbors

*Because your congregation is part of a
much larger body, others near and far will be available
to share their ideas and experiences with you.*

Chapter Six

You Don't Go It Alone

Therefore, since we are surrounded by so great a cloud of witnesses, let us also lay aside every weight and the sin that clings so closely, and let us run with perseverance the race that is set before us.

Hebrews 12:1

The role of the synod

The word *synod* (pronounced "SIN-ed," although it isn't about sin) comes from the Greek, meaning "fellow travelers," or more literally, "on the same road." The term has been used throughout church history to describe any group of Christian leaders who gather together from time to time to discuss common problems or reach joint decisions. In the Evangelical Lutheran Church in America, as in some of its predecessor bodies, the word *synod* is used to describe a number of congregations—usually those in a specific geographic area—that unite to accomplish those aspects of their ministry that would be difficult or impossible to accomplish separately.

Few congregations are large enough or blessed with sufficient resources to operate a college or seminary, a summer camp or retreat center, or a hospital or nursing home. Historically, these types of institutions were founded, owned, and controlled by synods. But recently, institutions and social service agencies of the church have become more independent from churches. Instead of being directly owned and controlled by the synod, they usually are separately incorporated non-profit organizations, often relating to several synods at once. However, the synod remains the organizational structure of the ELCA through which congregations support these ministries and have input into their governance.

As a "congregation of congregations," the synod has an annual meeting, just as your congregation does. Each congregation selects people, in addition to its pastors, to serve as voting members of the synod assembly. The synod assembly approves the synod's budget, conducts its necessary business as a corporation, and elects the synod's officers and members of key committees or boards. Among these is the synod council, which administers the synod's affairs between assemblies, just as your congregation council administers the affairs of the congregation between congregational meetings.

Another historical role for the synod has been to offer protection to congregations against false doctrines or misunderstandings of the faith. Synods exercised this protective role by examining candidates for ordained ministry, to ensure that people without proper training and a clear understanding of the gospel would not become pastors who would lead their congregations astray. Synods also maintained authority to discipline pastors or other congregation members whose teaching or behavior became disruptive, so that difficulties would not spread to neighboring congregations. Synods today continue in these roles by electing committees for consultation and for discipline, which follow procedures carefully outlined in the synod's own constitution and bylaws.

The leader of the synod is a member of the clergy elected to the office of bishop. In the New Testament, the term *bishop* often is used interchangeably with *pastor*, but over the centuries *bishop* has come to refer to a leader who holds an office of oversight over other pastors. In some denominational traditions that oversight is exercised quite directly, and bishops are very powerful. They appoint pastors to congregations at their pleasure, and dismiss pastors from congregations as they see fit.

F ind out which of the ELCA's 65 synods your congregation belongs to, where your synod office is located and how to contact the synod bishop or other staff members by visiting www.elca.org/sr.

In the Lutheran tradition in the United States, however, the power of bishops is limited to seeing that the various constitutional processes are followed for the calling of a pastor, and that the necessary procedures are adhered to when disciplinary actions become necessary. The actual exercise of discipline is carried out by the synod committees elected for that purpose. The bishop usually has one or more assistants, often clergy members, selected by the synod council. These assistants carry out various functions on the bishop's behalf, but they are not bishops of a lesser rank, as is the case in some denominations.

When a congregation is in need of a pastor, the potential candidates to fill the position would (at least theoretically) be ordained people on the clergy roster of the church, plus any other people who have met the various educational and spiritual requirements for ordination. In the ELCA, this includes more than 16,000 individuals. The bishop or the assistants work with the congregation's call committee to reduce this field to a more manageable number of candidates for serious consideration. It is a time-consuming process for congregations and pastors to discern God's will and seek the guidance of the Holy Spirit in bringing together the right pastor for each congregation. The synod helps this process run more smoothly.

Not only is the calling of a pastor an important decision for the pastor and the congregation most directly involved, it is also a decision with implications for neighboring congregations, as well. Because neighboring congregations often cooperate or overlap in their ministries—and because congregations share ministries together through participation in the synod—the decision to call a particular person to become the pastor of a congregation is not a decision that can be made in isolation. Therefore the advice of the synod staff in the call process helps assure that the pastor called to a congregation will not only be a good fit for the congregation but also will fit in well with colleagues serving neighboring parishes.

To assure that there is opportunity to consult about such matters and to share advice, and to attest that all legal and organizational requirements have been met in following proper procedures, the bishop must sign the official letter of call issued by the congregation to the candidate selected to become its pastor. This signature is a sign that the other congregations in the synod, who also are affected by the decision, agree with the congregation's choice of a candidate. Thus, the bishop's role in the call process is largely one of assisting the congregational call committee, and in representing the interests of the other congregations of the synod as the decision is made.

The churchwide organization

In addition to being part of a synod, your congregation is also part of the larger family of the denomination or "church body." The purpose of this body is not to control the congregation but rather to coordinate and carry out those ministries too large even for synods to undertake. While a synod might develop certain resources for worship or education, for example, it usually is not cost effective for a synod to publish its own hymnal or Sunday school curriculum. Similarly, while a synod—or even an individual congregation— might wish to sponsor a missionary being sent to some far off place, coordination is needed to see that a dozen missionaries are not sent to one nation while a nearby nation has none. Some tasks are too big even for synods, and require national or international coordination.

Like congregations and synods, the ELCA has regular meet-ings—not annual meetings, because they do not occur every year—but regular Churchwide Assemblies. Synod assemblies select people to serve as voting members of the Churchwide Assembly. The ELCA also has a Church Council elected by the Assembly to administer its affairs between assemblies. And the Assembly elects various boards and committees, made up of ordinary church members such as you, who make the day-to-day operating decisions concerning the vari-ous divisions, offices, commissions, and departments of the church

P eople sometimes refer to their entire denomination as "the national church," but this phrase is misleading for at least three reasons.

First, because the First Amendment to the U.S. Constitution guarantees the separation of church and state, the United States has no "national church."

Second, the Evangelical Lutheran Church in America, for exam-ple, includes members in North America who live outside the United States. ELCA congregations in Puerto Rico and the Virgin Islands are located on U.S. territory but are not actually part of the nation.

These are technicalities, but the biggest reason for not referring to the ELCA as "the national church" is that much of its scope actually is global. Mission work, world hunger programs, inter-national disaster response, membership in the Lutheran World Federation, dialogues with other church bodies of different denominational traditions, and many of the ELCA's other pri-mary activities really transcend national boundaries.

body. There is also a pastor, called the Presiding Bishop, elected by the Churchwide Assembly to preach, teach, and speak on behalf of the entire denomination.

Your congregation is a member of a congregation of congregations, as well as this larger church body. The congregation, synod, and churchwide organization all exist to nurture members like you in your faith, to provide the means necessary for the Church of Christ to carry out its mission and ministry, both locally and globally, and to witness to the unity we share in Jesus Christ.

Additional resources

One Great Cloud of Witnesses! You and Your Congregation in the Evangelical Lutheran Church in America, by Lowell G. Almen (Minneapolis: Augsburg Fortress, 1997). Includes more information on the idea of "congregation of congregations," especially on page 36.

Web sites

Evangelical Lutheran Church in America: www.elca.org

ELCA Department for Synodical Relations: www.elca.org/sr

Chapter Seven

Other Resources

This synod shall establish conferences, clusters, coalitions, or other area subdivisions within its territory as specified in the bylaws. The purpose of such groupings shall be to foster interdependent relationships among congregations, institutions, and synodical and churchwide units for mission purposes.

Constitution for Synods of the Evangelical Lutheran Church in America, edition revised as of August 13, 2001, provision S12.01.

Conferences, clusters or coalitions

Because some decisions in your congregation may affect neighboring congregations, leaders of different congregations often must work together. In some synods, a group of neighboring congregations is called a *conference.* In other synods, congregations that neighbor one another are referred to as a *cluster* of congregations. Still other synods organize neighboring congregations into *coalitions.* Whatever the term, these groupings acknowledge that congregations in the same neighborhood often face the same challenges and the same opportunities.

Some conferences, clusters, or coalitions are highly organized, incorporated ministries with paid staff and extensive programs. Others are simply informal gatherings that meet from time to time as they see fit. This varies greatly, not only from synod to synod but also among conferences or clusters within the same synod. In some areas congregations feel a need to formally band together, while in other areas congregations are comfortable just having a nodding acquaintanceship with the congregation down the road.

Conferences, clusters, and coalitions can be extremely useful for coordinating ministries among neighboring congregations so that ministries complement one another rather than compete with one another. Frequently, such groups can provide the means for congregations to share their particular strengths with one another and get help with ministry tasks in which they may be weaker. In urban areas where congregations may be as close as just a few blocks away from each other, cooperative ministries of this type are vital to providing a unified voice in proclaiming the gospel in word and deed to the neighborhood. In rural areas, where challenges are often great, cooperative ministries may be essential to survival.

Discover more about the conference, cluster, or coalition in your area. Learn how it is organized and what benefits it provides. If the cooperative ministry in your area is inactive, discuss how a group of neighboring congregations might work together to enhance the ministries of all. Then, if it seems appropriate, invite leaders of neighboring congregations to share in these discussions. There is strength in unity.

By the way, synods also sometimes need to work cooperatively with their neighbors, and are grouped into regions. The ELCA's 65 synods are grouped into nine geographic regions that help coordinate ministries that extend beyond synod boundaries. See www.elca.org/sr for a map of ELCA synods and regions.

Resource centers

Answers to frequently asked questions, solutions to common problems, and other resources are kept on file and available to congregations in places called resource centers. Some resource centers are little more than a file drawer in a synod office that is staffed by a part-time employee. Other resource centers are full libraries of books, audiotapes, videos, and other materials at centers staffed by teams of professionals serving multiple synods in a particular region. Whether the collection is rather modest or very extensive, these resources are available to you as a congregational leader as you carry out your assigned tasks in the ministry of your congregation.

ELCA mailings and Web sites

The ELCA also regularly distributes planning tips, ideas from other congregations, posters for upcoming churchwide emphases or events, samples of brochures and flyers available for purchase, and information about newly available resources for congregational ministries of all types. Ask your pastor or the administrative assistant at your church about the resources mailed to your congregation. Also visit the ELCA Web site at www.elca.org for online resources and information.

Not every question has an easy answer, and not every problem has been solved by others before you. Nevertheless, chances are that many of the challenges you face as a congregational leader have been met by others in similar circumstances. Because your congregation is part of a much larger body, others near and far will be available to share their ideas and experiences with you so that the whole body may be strengthened and lifted up. Just ask!

Y ou can find the location of the resource center for your synod by contacting your synod office, or by consulting the directory on the ELCA Web site. Go to www.elca.org and follow the links to "Resources" and then to "Resource centers." You also may direct your questions and problems to the ELCA's Resource Information Service by calling 800-638-3522 or by sending e-mail to info@elca.org.

PART IV

Strategies for Effective Leadership

*You can contribute your
leadership skills to help move tasks to
completion efficiently and pleasantly.*

Chapter Eight

Painless Meetings

The failure to plan is planning to fail.
American proverb

One thing that congregational leaders often complain about is having to attend meetings. Yet when done right, meetings can bring opportunities for fellowship, a sense of accomplishment, and sometimes even enjoyment. If you are the chairperson or are otherwise in charge of the meeting, you can do a great deal to make the event more enjoyable. But even if you aren't the designated leader of the meeting, you can contribute your leadership skills to help move tasks to completion efficiently and pleasantly.

Setting the agenda

The meetings people hate most are the ones that start out badly before they ever begin. If a meeting is not planned in advance, there is little likelihood that it will be an enjoyable experience. Even a "planning meeting" needs a plan! If you are the designated leader, begin with a sheet of paper where you can list exactly what must be accomplished at this meeting: What decisions must be made? What upcoming events must be planned or organized? What information will this group require in order to complete its tasks? What information does this group need to convey to others once it has finished its planning and decision-making?

Now ask yourself, "Is this meeting necessary?" If you have no decisions to make, no plans to initiate, or if the decisions can be made more easily without a meeting (perhaps by simply phoning the members of the group and asking for their approval), by all means cancel the meeting! There is nothing people despise more than being asked to waste their time by attending a meeting that has no purpose. Yet countless meetings are held in congregations month after month in which more time is spent with refreshments than on necessary business. If the decisions are few and can wait until next month, blessed are you when you postpone the meeting until the agenda can be full.

Speaking of agendas, once you have prepared your list of reasons to meet, decisions that are pending, and plans that need to be made, organize the list in an orderly fashion, placing the most urgent business first, and leaving the least urgent business to the last. With the widespread availability of computers and photocopy machines, it should be a simple matter to type up an agenda and make a copy for each member of the group. The agenda should be detailed enough for group members to see what topics will be considered and what actions will need to be taken. However, no agenda should require more than one side of a single sheet of paper.

Put the date, time, and place of the meeting at the top of the agenda. If possible, send a copy of the agenda to each member of the group a few days in advance. This not only reminds them of them of

Although it is true that meetings should be accomplished quickly and efficiently, you nevertheless are part of a community of spiritual formation that nurtures the faith. So take time at the beginning of your meeting for some brief devotions, and end your meeting with prayer. Put these on the agenda—they are part of the plan. (See chapter 13 for more on including devotions and prayer in your meetings.)

the meeting but it testifies to the meeting's importance. Attendance problems usually disappear when members are reminded in a timely fashion, and when they see that the meeting has a purpose and a plan.

When you meet, start the meeting promptly at the time that was announced. If your group gets in the habit of starting 10 minutes late, it won't be long before group members begin arriving 10 minutes late. After a few meetings, you won't get started until 20 minutes after the appointed time. Respect the fact that group members have other commitments and that their time is valuable. Begin on time and end within 60 to 90 minutes. If a meeting will require more than one full hour (excluding devotional or study time, refreshments, and socializing), it is likely you will no longer have the full attention and concentration of members. Leave the unfinished business for next month, or set a special meeting. Again, attendance problems are less likely when expectations are reasonable, group members can anticipate consistent meeting length, and the value of their time is appreciated.

A short course in small group communication

The key to success as part of a council, committee, board, or task group is largely a matter of striking a balance between accomplishing the necessary tasks and maintaining the satisfaction of group members. To err on the side of being task-oriented will probably get things done, but group members might find the experience very unsatisfying. They could even become angry or resentful. On the other hand, paying too much attention to making sure everyone is having a good time may mean that the important tasks are never accomplished.

Corporations often oversee groups through a threat of punishment. If group members do not attend meetings and accomplish their tasks, they may receive poor evaluations, be denied raises or promotions, or even lose their jobs. Voluntary associations, meanwhile, rely on promised rewards to maintain groups. If group members do not enjoy the company of other members, find fulfillment in achieving the tasks before them, or receive recognition and appreciation of some sort for what they do, they may choose to withdraw from the group or quit the association entirely. Congregational groups are maintained, therefore, with rewards rather than punishments.

Accomplishing tasks while maintaining group satisfaction can be a delicate balancing act. How can a leader know the right path to take? Group leaders must develop a sense for when it's time to stop to talk about what's happening in members' lives, and when it's time to press forward with the next item on the agenda. They have to learn when it's time for a laugh and when concentrated seriousness is required. The trick is to get things done but to have a good experience while doing it. If the group is all business and no fellowship, satisfaction is likely to fall in the short term. But if the group is all about enjoying one another's company and never accomplishes anything, satisfaction is likely to fall in the long term.

The fact is that no individual can lead a group singlehandedly! We all have different gifts to contribute to the whole. This is particularly true in a group meeting. Even if one person happens to be the designated leader or chairperson, the leadership of the group is a function of the entire group.

Identifying task roles

All group members contribute to the group's leadership by fulfilling certain functional leadership roles. More than 50 years ago, scholars studying small group communication identified task roles and maintenance roles within groups. Task roles relate to accomplishing tasks, while maintenance roles deal with maintaining group satisfaction. A summary of these roles appears in Tables 1 and 2 on pages 52-53.

Some designated leaders are particularly task-oriented. Their set of gifts makes them best suited for functioning in some of the roles on Table 1. Group members help these task-oriented designated leaders by filling in the gaps with other gifts, particularly by functioning in some of the roles on Table 2. On the other hand, some designated leaders tend to be more maintenance-oriented. Their gifts make them inclined to fulfill roles on Table 2. Group members help these leaders by supplying gifts and fulfilling roles on Table 1. No one possesses all of the gifts necessary to fulfill every role. Group members play different roles at different times, as appropriate, but all contribute to the roles necessary to lead the group. So if a group becomes either too task-oriented or too maintenance-oriented, the designated leader is not the only one to blame. It is up to all members of the group to contribute to its leadership.

No one possesses all of the gifts necessary to fulfill every role.

Look over the descriptions of the leadership roles in Table 1 and Table 2. Which roles do you most often find yourself fulfilling in a group? Which roles could you comfortably step into more often? Which roles are you least comfortable fulfilling? On which table— *task* or *maintenance*—do you find the greater number of roles with which you are most comfortable? Do you tend to be more of a task-oriented person, or more maintenance-oriented? Check your perceptions of yourself with someone else.

Table 1	Group task roles
Initiator/contributor	Suggests or proposes new ideas or approaches to a goal or a problem facing the group.
Information seeker	Asks for clarification of suggestions that others made. Asks for information and facts pertinent to the topic at hand.
Information giver	Offers clarifications, facts, or experiences directly related to the topic being discussed.
Opinion seeker	Asks for a clarification of the values the group is using to judge suggestions or alternatives.
Opinion giver	States personal beliefs or opinions concerning suggestions or alternatives currently being considered by the group.
Elaborator	Spells out suggestions in terms of examples or meanings developed by the group. Offers a rationale for suggestions that were previously made and tries to explain how ideas or suggestions would work out if adopted by the group.
Coordinator	Tries to pull ideas and suggestions together or tries to coordinate the activities of various members. Clarifies the relationships among different ideas and suggestions.
Orienter	Defines the position of the group with respect to its goals by summarizing what has occurred. Points out departures from agreed-upon directions or objectives. Raises questions about where the group discussion is going.
Evaluator/critic	Evaluates or questions the practicality, logic, facts, or procedure of a suggestion or of the group discussion. This "devil's advocate" plays a vital role for the group.
Energizer	Prods the group to action or decision. Attempts to motivate the group to a greater or higher quality of activity.
Procedural technician	Expedites group process by performing routine tasks. (For example, distributing materials, rearranging the seating, or running audiovisual equipment.)
Recorder	Writes down suggestions, group decisions, or outcomes of discussion. Functions as the "group memory."

Table 2	Group maintenance roles
Encourager	Praises, agrees with, and accepts the contribution of others. Indicates warmth and solidarity toward other group members. Offers commendation and, in various ways, indicates understanding and acceptance of other points of view, ideas, and suggestions.
Harmonizer	Mediates the differences between other members. Attempts to reconcile disagreements. Relieves tension in conflict situations through humor or "pouring oil on troubled waters."
Compromiser	May offer steps toward compromise by yielding status, admitting errors, or meeting people halfway.
Gatekeeper and expediter	Attempts to keep communication channels open by encouraging or facilitating the participation of others (such as, "We haven't heard Carol's ideas yet") or by proposing regulations to improve the flow of communication. (For example, "Why don't we limit the length of our contributions so that we can hear from everyone?")
Standard setter	Expresses standards for the group to attempt to achieve in its functioning or applies standards in evaluating the quality of group processes. (For example, "We should really keep working until we find a solution that will be acceptable to the youth as well as to the retirees.")
Group observer and commentator	Keeps records of various aspects of group process, and provides this information and interpretations into the group's evaluation of its own procedures.
Follower	Goes along with the direction of the group, accepting the ideas of others and listening carefully during group discussions.

Tables 1 and 2 are adapted from Kenneth D. Benne and Paul Sheats, "Functional Roles of Group Members," *The Journal of Social Issues*, vol. IV, no. 2 (Spring 1948), pp. 41-49.

Chapter Nine

The Decision-Making Process

The more abstract the proposition under consideration, the greater the possibilities of joint agreement; and the more concrete the proposition under consideration, the less the opportunity for full agreement.

John W. Keltner, *Interpersonal Speech-Communication: Element and Structures* (Wadsworth, 1970), p. 153

Whether your council, committee, board, or task group is planning a worship service or confronting the challenge of a leaking roof, the process of deliberation and decision-making will follow a similar pattern—and will face similar pitfalls at each step along the way. Understanding the process groups use in making decisions will help you participate more effectively and sense when the group's course needs to change in order to get back on track.

Discern the task or problem

The first challenge in making any decision is to define the problem clearly: What is the overall objective? What would be the best possible outcome? What obstacles are in the way of achieving this objective or outcome? What decisions must be made first? What decisions have already been made? What specifically must be decided at this step? If the situation is complex, it may be necessary to break it down into a series of problems that can be handled one at a time. Make sure all members of your group understand and agree upon the problem that needs to be dealt with and the obstacles that stand between you and your goal, before beginning deliberation.

This part sounds easy, but groups often waste considerable time trying to solve the wrong problem or by having several problems on the table at once. Select the top problem that must be addressed right now, deal with it alone, then move on to the next decision that must be made. Decisions can always be revisited later if the solution to a later problem calls into question something that was sorted out earlier. So decide what the problem of the moment must be and make sure all group members understand that this is the decision you are making now.

For example, when the topic of the annual Easter Sunday breakfast is brought up, it's likely that one person in the group will want to jump into deciding the menu while another person worries about how much the suggested donation should be. Meanwhile, someone else will be ready to discuss the centerpieces for the tables, and yet another person will ask why there should be a breakfast on Easter at all. Somehow those questions must be arranged from the most general (Why are we doing this? What is the goal?) down to the most specific (What will we serve? How will we decorate?). Each question has to be considered and decided before moving on to the next. Only in this way can you avoid chaos in the decision-making process, and also ensure that the centerpieces relate to the theme! So make sure you are all working on the same question, the right question, and one question at a time.

Generate possible solutions

Next, begin a list of possible solutions. Sometimes the available options are very few and have an obvious "yes" or "no" response. But other times the group must generate its own set of possible alternatives. A chalkboard or a large piece of paper on the wall can help group members visualize a long list of possibilities. It's best to be open-minded at this point. Sometimes a bizarre suggestion, or even something suggested as a joke, can trigger a creative idea from someone else. Keep the ideas flowing and get everyone to contribute.

Test the possibilities and gather consensus

When the flow of possible solutions is exhausted, go back over the list and test each suggestion. This is the time to scrutinize each idea carefully. The criteria you use to evaluate each suggestion will usually be fairly obvious: Which of these alternatives will best accomplish the stated goal? But if you notice the tests changing as you go through the list, it might be a good idea to go back and reconsider earlier suggestions based on the emerging criteria.

Eventually your group probably will gain consensus around a particular solution or course of action. When a decision can't be reached, it is usually because the question before the group needs to be broken down into several questions. In this case, it's best to go back to the beginning, redefine the problem and generate a new list of possible solutions.

Delegate with accountability and support

Once a particular course of action has been decided upon, the group needs to break down the steps necessary to complete the project and achieve the goal. A simple planning grid will allow the individual tasks to be listed and prioritized. Then each task can be assigned to one or more people who will receive what they need for their duties, follow through on their assignment, and let a designated leader know that the task is complete. The key in this step is to delegate tasks clearly so that each person receiving an

Sample planning grid

Task	Date due	Resources needed	Person responsible	Reports to:
Get commitment from keynote speaker	March 15	List of possible speakers	Bill	Christine
Send news release to local paper	April 3	Name and bio of keynote speaker	Christine	Pastor

assignment knows precisely what it is that must be done, when their part of the project must be completed, and to whom they are to report when they are finished—or to whom they are to turn when they run into problems. The potential pitfalls here are that someone may accept a delegated task without understanding it. This is when things "fall through the cracks."

Complete a thorough evaluation and assessment

A final step in any successful planning process—but a step that too often is overlooked or bypassed—is evaluation and assessment. Whenever your group completes a project, large or small, you should take time to evaluate how things went. Was the course of action the right one, or would a different solution to the problem have worked better? Were delegations clear? Did people have what they needed in order to follow through? What was left out? What went really well?

The purpose of the final assessment is not to lay blame but to learn from mistakes so that the group's job can be done more effectively in the future. When a job is well done, a final evaluation helps contribute to group maintenance by providing a time for well-deserved congratulations. If the project involved some event that will be repeated, perhaps at the same time next year, it can be very helpful to record the group's self assessment in writing and to keep the record in a file for future planning.

When group members approach the decision-making process unaware of these steps, they often stumble through the process in a haphazard fashion. When group members are consciously aware of these steps, meetings can go quickly, tasks can be accomplished efficiently, and the group members can gain a feeling of satisfaction from a job well done.

Robert's Rules

Some new leaders feel unqualified to serve their congregations on councils, boards, committees, or task groups because they are uncomfortable with the "parliamentary procedures" used in conducting meetings. Parliamentary procedure is a set of rules that have been developed gradually over many, many years. As the name implies, these rules evolved from the English Parliament. They are used today in Congress, state legislatures, other government bodies, and almost universally at formal meetings. They are recorded in a rather intimidating book, available in most bookstores, called *Robert's Rules of Order.*

Parliamentary rules really are designed for meetings of large groups, or meetings that are highly contentious. When your entire congregation meets, or your synod assembles, those are fairly large groups, and parliamentary rules will help those meetings run

Five steps to successful group projects

1. Discern the task or problem.

2. Generate possible solutions.

3. Test the possibilities and gather consensus around one course of action.

4. Delegate the tasks with accountability and adequate support.

5. Complete a thorough evaluation and assessment.

smoothly. Your congregation council and other planning groups in the congregation, however, should neither be large nor contentious. Rather than picking over points of order and counting votes, these groups should be conducting respectful and civil discussions leading toward consensus of the entire group.

If it is necessary in a particular situation to adhere to Robert's Rules, many guides are available. The important thing to remember is that the rules are intended to help groups discuss topics, make decisions, and get things done. It is far more important to have the discussion and make the decision than it is to strictly follow the rules. If formal rules aren't absolutely required to make the meeting work, it's better to simply concentrate on maintaining the group through mutual respect and common courtesy.

Additional resources

Our Structure: Carrying Out the Vision, by Brian H. Hughes (Minneapolis: Augsburg Fortress, 2002).

PART V

Sharing the Load

*When you invite a potential volunteer to use
his or her abilities in a particular service to the congregation,
you are offering an opportunity to respond to the
gracious love of Christ.*

Chapter Ten

Enlisting and Encouraging Volunteers

I believe that there is on earth a holy little flock and community of pure saints under one head, Christ. It is called together by the Holy Spirit in one faith, mind and understanding. It possesses a variety of gifts, and yet is united in love without sect or schism. Of this community I also am a part and member, a participant and co-partner in all the blessings it possesses.

Robert Kolb and Timothy J. Wengert,
Large Catechism, *The Book of Concord*, pp. 437-438

Seldom is a congregational board, committee, or task force expected to plan, arrange, and carry out a major project all by itself. Congregations regularly recruit volunteers for a variety of tasks— everything from washing communion ware after worship to teaching Sunday school, and from painting walls to sewing quilts to singing in a choir. Because congregations are voluntary associations, nearly everything is accomplished by volunteers, and the work of many volunteers consists of finding still more volunteers! Here are just a few brief tips on how to go about the sometimes daunting task of finding the volunteers needed to carry out your congregation's ministry.

Discerning the gifts of others

As you consider the volunteers you need to recruit for a given task, begin by giving some thought to the gifts you have observed in other members of your congregation. Don't just think about what "warm bodies" you can arm-twist into the job, but think about who would be well suited for the particular task. Who would be good at this? Who would find this task satisfying and might derive a sense of accomplishment from participating in it?

Sometimes it can be helpful to sit down with a list of church members or a congregational directory—a pictorial directory is even better, if available—and give some thought to each name in terms of matching gifts to the task at hand. When volunteers are asked to use their unique gifts, they are far more likely to say yes. Some congregations routinely distribute a "gifts inventory" sheet through which members may respond and let congregational leaders know in what ways they feel they can best serve the church. If a collection of such sheets is available to you, this is an excellent resource for matching the gifts of potential volunteers to those needed for a certain task.

Rather than recruiting those individuals who are already heavily involved in many ways in the congregation's work, look for people who may be near the fringes, but for whom this task would be a special opportunity to utilize their gifts. While some people remain at the edges of congregational involvement by choice, others do so because they are shy, or because they lack self-confidence in their abilities. Still others are simply waiting to be invited! Recruiting volunteers is an opportunity to draw them into the fellowship of the congregation.

Offering opportunities, not obligations

The next step is to contact each individual in as personal a manner as is practical and invite him or her to take on this opportunity to serve. Please go back and read that last sentence once again—the words in it were chosen very carefully!

Potential volunteers should be contacted in as personal a manner as is practical. In some cases you may be attempting to recruit a large number of volunteers, and you might be tempted to simply send a form letter to everyone on your list. Because a form letter can be impersonal, many potential volunteers will be inclined to simply throw it away. It is more difficult to throw away a handwritten note addressed specifically to that person. It is still more difficult to hang up on another member who has called on the telephone. And it is most difficult of all to walk away from someone who is issuing an invitation face to face. If the number of volunteers needed is too large to recruit each one personally, perhaps the first step ought to be to recruit volunteers who are willing to help recruit other volunteers, so that each person receives a personal invitation.

Invite is an important word. While it might seem expedient to do a bit of arm-twisting, it's almost never to the congregation's advantage to try to coerce or trap people into giving their time. Invitations to service, with generous encouragement, are similar to Christ's invitation to the disciples: "Follow me." Some people accepted that invitation immediately (Matthew 4:18-22; Mark 2:14) and others were reluctant at first (Matthew 8:18-22; Luke 18:18-23). But Jesus never coerced or forced anyone to become a disciple, he only issued invitations and allowed the invited person to respond.

Honestly and briefly tell the potential volunteer something about the task at hand, and what gifts you have seen in that person that caused you to think of him or her for the job. When you tell potential volunteers that you thought of them because you've seen how good they are at some closely related activity, hopefully you are not engaging in idle flattery but are genuinely helping another member of Christ's family to identify and affirm her spiritual gifts. When you tell someone that you have a job that requires certain skills, and that you know he possesses those skills, you affirm his gifts and offer a Christ-like invitation to serve.

When you invite a potential volunteer to use his or her abilities in a particular service to the congregation, you are offering an opportunity to respond to the gracious love of Christ. You do not

place before that person a test to be passed or failed, but a chance
to give back to God in thanksgiving for God's mercy.

Don't say "no" for them

Just as you would not say "yes" for that potential volunteer by
forcing or coercing a response, neither should you say "no" for that
person by not offering the opportunity. When considering others
for a task, we sometimes decide not to ask them to serve because
we are able to think of the various excuses that person might offer
us by way of refusal. If we don't issue the invitation, it is as if we
refused the call to discipleship on behalf of that person, without
their knowledge.

If you catch yourself saying, "Oh, I won't ask Jane to do this, she
is so busy with her new baby!" or "This won't be a good time to
approach John, he hasn't been feeling well lately," you are no longer
evaluating that person's gifts for the task. Instead, you are making
excuses for them (or excusing yourself from issuing an invitation to
that person). It just may be that Jane really needs a diversion from
the stress of a new family, or that John's illness has left him feeling
lonely and as a result more eager to get involved. Extend the invitation, and let them decide for themselves whether or not this is a
good time and place to serve.

Recruiting volunteers is about matching gifts to tasks, and about
offering invitations to serve, rather than making others feel oblig-
ated or guilty about refusing.

Additional resources

Our Gifts: Identifying and Developing Leaders, by David Mayer
(Minneapolis: Augsburg Fortress, 2002).

Our Structure: Carrying Out the Vision, by Brian H. Hughes
(Minneapolis: Augsburg Fortress, 2002).

Chapter Eleven

Keeping Others in the Loop

This is the covenant that I will make with the house of Israel after those days, says the Lord: I will put my laws in their minds, and write them on their hearts, and I will be their God, and they shall be my people. And they shall not teach one another or say to each other, "Know the Lord," for they shall all know me, from the least of them to the greatest.

Hebrews 8:10-11

On the day that this prophecy is fulfilled, we shall no longer need to master communication skills. In the meantime, however, intentional communication is absolutely vital. There are other people in your congregation and community who have the right to know, the need to know, or even an obligation to know about the decisions and actions of your council, board, committee, or task group. The only way these people can find out what they should know is if you tell them.

Communicating with pastors, staff, the council, and other groups

Pastors, staff members, and other key congregational leaders need to know what each decision-making and planning group is up to. It is the job of the pastor and congregation council members to coordinate all of the activities of the congregation and to ensure that the congregation "speaks with one voice." In wanting to know about the actions of your group, your pastor or congregational president is not being "nosy" or acting like a "control freak." Rather, he or she is fulfilling a responsibility to be aware of the full range of the congregation's ministries. Key leaders cannot support your decisions or explain them to others if they are kept in the dark.

The bylaws of many congregations provide for the pastors to have *ex officio* membership on all councils, committees, and boards of the congregation. The purpose is to provide the most direct line of communication between the decision-making group and the pastor. Pastors, however, seldom have the time to be at every meeting of every group. This means that a written record of your group's actions needs to be made and circulated to the congregation's key leaders.

Except for meetings of the congregation council and entire congregation, formal minutes usually are not necessary for most other types of meetings. However, having one member of a planning group responsible for taking important notes can help maintain a record for the group and keep key leaders informed. Because your group will always have a written agenda, simply noting the agenda items and the actions taken on each item usually is adequate.

A simple form might be sufficient this purpose, similar to the one shown on page 68. The form can fit on a half sheet of paper, or the agenda itself might be prepared with adequate space for notes. The form or annotated agenda may then be photocopied for the pastor(s), council president, or others who have a need to know of your group's actions. Such a form may also serve to help your group communicate internally in the form of a record that can be filed and referred to later to help you recall certain actions or decisions.

Communicating with the whole congregation

No matter what the responsibilities of your group are, you carry them out on behalf of the whole congregation and in the congregation's name. Therefore, all members of the congregation have a stake in your activities. Although the congregation as a whole does not need to know the details of every action your group takes, this information should be available to those who are interested. Always be open and forthright in responding to questions about your group. Sooner or later, your group will make a bad decision. You are human, after all—and humans inevitably make mistakes. When this occurs, don't try to hide the error, and don't try to dodge the responsibility. Simply explain what happened, what you have learned from it, and how you are taking steps to ensure that things will go better next time. Confession and forgiveness are not just good theology, they also are good practice in group communication.

From time to time your group will need to report highlights of its activities, perhaps in an annual report or other congregational document. Keep the report brief and to the point, without exaggerating accomplishments or embellishing them with flowery language. Use bullet points to list your accomplishments so people can identify them easily. Include charts or graphs when they will communicate complicated information more clearly than paragraphs of text. Make it easy for congregation members to get the big picture of what your group has done and is doing.

If you wish to encourage others in the congregation to participate in an event or activity planned by your group, start early. Begin to get the word out at least a month prior to the date of the event. Use whatever media are at your disposal—bulletins, newsletters, verbal announcements, and even special mailings (if the event justifies the expense). Make sure each and every announcement addresses the classic "Five Ws and an H": WHO, WHAT, WHEN, WHERE, WHY, and HOW. Here is an example:

> Confirmands and their families (WHO) are invited to a potluck supper (WHAT) on Wednesday, September 10, at 6:30 P.M. (WHEN) in the church fellowship hall (WHERE). Come learn about confirmation classes and activities for the year (WHY). Bring your own table service and a salad, hot dish, or dessert to share. Beverages will be provided (HOW).

Sample communication form or annotated agenda

Meeting of the Worship Committee October 7	
Agenda Item	**Action**
1. Thanksgiving Eve Service	Finalized liturgy outline and hymns. Recommend council designates offering to the World Hunger Appeal.
2. Christ the King Sunday	Will use *Lutheran Book of Worship*, Setting 2. Extra assistants needed for procession—Phil will recruit these.
3. Advent Worship	Will use *With One Voice* hymnal, Setting 4. Paul will set up Advent wreath, Laura will contact families for each week's lighting ceremony.
4. Christmas Eve	Need input on theme from pastor—James will contact her. Sue will check with office secretary about ordering bulletin covers.

Don't be afraid of repetition. Research shows that an individual usually must receive a message seven to nine times before it really sinks in. So even if the message is published in a weekly newsletter, Sunday bulletins, and verbal announcements each week (three different media each week), it will take a minimum of three weeks to send the message to everyone nine times. Further, the most effective messages use more than one of the senses to grab audience attention. A mix of verbal and written announcements, and visual aids, will help to get the message across.

Look at the advertising industry for examples of how to promote an event or activity. Advertisers use short messages, carefully crafted to capture the attention of the audience and repeated time and again. Follow the same formula in promoting events to members of your congregation.

Communicating beyond the congregation

Your congregation is a great place, with friendly people, important activities, and the greatest message in the world to proclaim! You know that . . . but do your neighbors know it? The most effective proclamation of the good news is still done one on one. The best way to invite someone to church is face to face. But in our fast-paced, media-saturated society, we often don't know our neighbors as well as people did in previous generations. We may need a little help getting people in the community close enough to be within range of personal witness and individual invitations.

With a bit of imagination, you can find many ways to tell your congregation's story to a wider audience and invite the neighbors to come and learn more. At the very least, you should see to it that whenever your congregation plans an event that is just a bit out of the ordinary, or that may be of interest to any person outside the congregation, that local news organizations are notified (newspapers, magazines, radio stations, TV stations). This notification takes the form of a *news release*. A news release is an announcement to an editor or news director so they might cover your event. If possible, send the release to the editor or director by name. Make sure they have it one week or two weeks before the event.

To see what to include in a news release, look at the front page of your local newspaper. Each story is preceded by a headline that briefly describes the event. Check the writing style in the first few paragraphs of the front-page stories. Most of the stories will be direct and to the point, emphasizing WHO, WHAT, WHEN, WHERE, WHY, and HOW. Put your news release on church letter-head, double-spaced, and make sure to include your name and phone number, or the name and number a reporter can use to get

Various media can help point others to your congregation and the activities and programs that take place there. Most congregations have a sign out front. Too often, though, such signs are poorly placed, too small to be read by passing traffic, poorly lit, or have no space for promoting current events. But if you can use a church sign to promote an event, do so.

Brochures or flyers delivered door to door by volunteers can be inexpensive and effective. Mailings to every household in the neighborhood are more costly and less personal, but they can get the message across, too.

Billboards or other outdoor advertising in high-traffic areas call attention to your congregation if used properly.

Newspapers in small communities are often hungry for local news, and will publish news of coming events for free if the information is packaged in a form that is easy for them to use.

Local radio or TV stations may see what your congregation is doing as news to be covered and aired.

more information. Keep your announcement short—usually a single page is best. A bit of free publicity for the gospel and for your congregation is worth the effort and if it makes the news, your story just might interest someone in the audience who is ready for an invitation to discipleship.

Additional resources

Go Public! Developing Your Plan for Communication Evangelism: A Guide for Congregations, by Mark D. Johns (Minneapolis: Augsburg Fortress, 1998).

Our Staff: Building Our Human Resources, by Trish Holford (Minneapolis: Augsburg Fortress, 2002).

Chapter Twelve

When Conflict Occurs

If another member of the church sins against you, go and point out the fault when the two of you are alone. If the member listens to you, you have regained that one. But if you are not listened to, take one or two others along with you, so that every word may be confirmed by the evidence of two or three witnesses. If the member refuses to listen to them, tell it to the church; and if the offender refuses to listen even to the church, let such a one be to you as a Gentile and a tax collector.

Matthew 18:15-17

Whether they are conscious of it or not, people who gather together in a group to make decisions or solve problems usually will go through four basic stages.

1. At first, group members will be cautious and courteous.

2. As they get to know one another and note differences in attitudes or approaches to the topic under consideration, group members will become more argumentative. They may state their positions vigorously or challenge one another's ideas strongly.

3. In time, group members begin to resolve these conflicts and establish rules (often unspoken) for how they will get along despite their differences.

4. Finally, group members begin to work toward compromise and consensus, focusing on the decisions they must make and the problems they must solve.

Healthy and unhealthy conflict

What this analysis of small group development tells us is that a certain amount of conflict is inevitable in all decision-making groups. Disagreements, heated debates, and even arguments are part of the natural course of group development. So when they occur, we should not assume that the group has failed. Indeed, conflict may signal that the group is on its way to its most productive stage. But conflict can be healthy or unhealthy, and the ways in which group members respond to conflict may be helpful or counterproductive.

Conflict is healthy when it involves genuine differences of opinion about which decision and course of action will best achieve the group's goal. Group members respond positively to conflicts when they respect the other people even while disagreeing with their opinions. When experienced in this way, conflict can lead to rigorous weighing of the merits of various options and careful discernment among courses of action.

Conflict is unhealthy when it involves maneuvering for power, attempting to dominate the group, or attacking people's personalities. When a group member uses conflict to get revenge for some perceived past slight, or to block an action simply because the member did not get his or her way, conflict becomes an obstacle to the accomplishment of the group's tasks and makes maintenance of group satisfaction difficult. Even worse, a group member may bring anger about issues at home or work to a group meeting, and direct that anger toward group activities. This leaves the other group members hurt and confused.

Group members do not need to avoid conflict when it emerges. But they do need to ask themselves, "What is the source of this conflict? Is it about the issues, or is it about personalities? Is our response to it healthy and constructive, or is this conflict leading us away from our goals?" If everyone continues to monitor the conflict in this way, by practicing mutual respect and self-control, conflict can actually be helpful. When conflict turns unhealthy, group members must step in, using the roles of harmonizer and compromiser, to soften the conflict.

A biblical model

Jesus understood human nature and knew that conflict among his disciples would surely occur. In Matthew 18:15-17, note that Jesus does not counsel his disciples to avoid conflict, but to directly confront those in the congregation who create conflict that is needless or hurtful. Jesus does not differentiate between harm caused by words or by deeds.

That confrontation of wrongdoing begins privately. Because our careless words or deeds can hurt people unintentionally, the person who has been wronged makes the first move toward reconciliation. It requires considerable courage to take this risk.

Conflict cannot be put to rest until it is dealt with. Yet the risks involved in not confronting the wrongdoer are even greater. If the person is not confronted, the conflict can continue to affect future interactions between those involved. Conflict cannot be put to rest until it is dealt with.

Because most conflict begins unintentionally, the private confrontation is generally sufficient to point out the problem and to lead to confession or apology and reconciliation.

The longer conflict continues, the more difficult it is to resolve. It is no favor to anyone to pretend the harsh word was never spoken, or that the hurtful deed was never done. Whenever one is mistreated by another, it is imperative that the conflict be confronted and resolved as soon as possible. When conflicts simmer beneath the surface over long periods of time, they can erupt in unexpected ways.

Congregations with long-standing conflicts may need assistance in working through a process of reconciliation. Contact your synod staff or synod Consultation Committee for this type of assistance.

Additional resources

Our Community: Dealing with Conflict in Our Congregation, by Susan M. Lang (Minneapolis: Augsburg Fortress, 2002).

PART VI

Maintaining Spiritual Foundations

Your congregation is not actually "yours."
Rather, it belongs to Christ and falls under
the leadership of the Holy Spirit.

Chapter 13

Remembering Why We're Doing What We're Doing

For no one can lay any foundation other than the one that has been laid; that foundation is Jesus Christ.

1 Corinthians 3:11

In previous chapters, much has been said about constitutions and bylaws, meeting agendas and functional roles, decision-making processes and conflicts. All of these are important topics, and in a book of this size there is space only to scratch the surface. Yet most of these things are functions of your congregation's existence as a voluntary association or as a non-profit organization. It is easy to get caught up in the system of organization or the relationships of an association and to forget that your congregation is a community of spiritual formation.

Opportunities for spiritual growth

Above all, your congregation is called by the Holy Spirit and through the gospel. As you meet in the various groups to which you have been appointed or elected, and as you perform all of the vital tasks necessary to fulfill organizational goals and maintain a harmonious association, take a few minutes simply to be a community in study and in prayer. In our busy-ness to get the congregation's work done, moments of devotion and attention to the scriptures can easily be swept aside or forgotten.

Group devotions need not be a burden. Indeed, they should be a joy! The designated leader of the group need not be the devotional leader. This task may be delegated to others in the group, perhaps with each taking a turn from one meeting to the next. Make up a schedule at the beginning of each year, then note on the agenda which person will lead the devotions at the meeting, as a reminder.

Many excellent devotional guides for congregational groups are available. These guides often combine opportunities for study and discussion, along with readings and prayers. Whatever resources for study and devotion your group chooses, make it a priority to include time for this at each meeting. It's well worth the investment in order to keep your group focused on that which is most central.

Make it a priority to include opportunities for spiritual growth in your personal routine as well. Guides for personal devotions might be available already at your church, or you can purchase your own. Reading the Bible, spending time in prayer, worshiping regularly, and participating in Christian education classes can give you opportunities to grow in your faith and to grow as a congregational leader.

Additional resources

Growing Together: Spiritual Exercises for Church Committees, by Rochelle Melander and Harold Eppley (Minneapolis: Augsburg Fortress, 1998).

Devotionals for individuals and families

Subscriptions for three devotionals are available through Augsburg Fortress: *Christ in Our Home*, *The Word in Season*, and *The Home Altar* (a devotional for families with children).

Chapter 14

A Word of Encouragement

Although I am the very least of all the saints, this grace was given to me to bring to the Gentiles the news of the boundless riches of Christ, and to make everyone see what is the plan of the mystery hidden for ages in God who created all things; so that through the church the wisdom of God in its rich variety might now be made known to the rulers and authorities in the heavenly places.

Ephesians 3:8-10

Congregational leadership can seem like an impossible task. Congregations are complex collections of people and organizational structures. There are many things to think about, anticipate, plan, and react to every time congregation members gather together for nearly any purpose at all.

This complexity makes serving as a congregational leader challenging. Who can possibly do everything? As we've seen, no one person can excel in all aspects of leadership. Leadership is the combination of gifts that all members bring. Leadership belongs to the whole church, and grows from our interactions with one another. You are not expected to know, and do, and be everything as a leader, but simply to contribute the gifts God has given you for leadership, trusting that God will use them to the greater good of all.

As a congregational leader, you follow a path traveled by many others before you. For almost 2,000 years, Christian congregations have faced these same challenges. Other leaders, no more or less talented than those of today, have served in their congregations during good times and bad, and carried out the mission and ministry of the church in their time and place.

As you take your place in this long procession of leaders, remember that ultimately your congregation is not actually "yours." Rather, it belongs to Christ and falls under the leadership of the Holy Spirit. If you are faithful in using all of your gifts to the full extent you are able and carrying out your leadership responsibilities to the best of your ability, you can trust God to see to it that your efforts will bear fruit for the gospel. The God who has claimed you and blessed you with good gifts, and the members of your congregation who have placed you in this position of leadership, have every confidence in you. You are a child of God!

You can trust God to see to it that your efforts will bear fruit for the gospel.